SCRATCH
CHALLENGE
WORKBOOK

Written by Steve Setford & Craig Steele

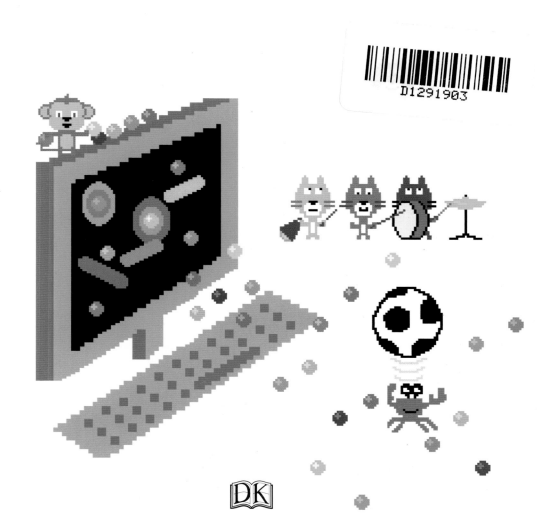

DK

Written by
Steve Setford & Craig Steele
Editor Steve Setford
Designer Peter Radcliffe
US Editor Allison Singer
Jacket Coordinator Francesca Young
Jacket Designers Dheeraj Arora, Amy Keast
Managing Editor Laura Gilbert
Managing Art Editor Diane Peyton Jones
Pre-Production Producer Nikoleta Parasaki
Producer Niamh Tierney
Art Director Martin Wilson
Publisher Sarah Larter
Publishing Director Sophie Mitchell

First American Edition, 2017
Published in the United States by DK Publishing
345 Hudson Street, New York, New York 10014

Copyright © 2017 Dorling Kindersley Limited
DK, a Division of Penguin Random House LLC
17 18 19 20 21 10 9 8 7 6 5 4 3 2 1
001–298651–Feb/2017

A catalog record for this book
is available from the Library of Congress.
ISBN: 978-1-4654-5686-1

DK books are available at special discounts when purchased
in bulk for sales promotions, premiums, fund-raising, or
educational use. For details, contact DK Publishing Special
Markets, 345 Hudson Street, New York, New York 10014
SpecialSales@dk.com

Scratch is developed by the Lifelong Kintergarten Group at
MIT Media Lab. See http://scratch.mit.edu

Picture Credits
The publisher would like to thank the following for their kind
permission to reproduce their photographs:
(Key: c-center; l-left; r-right)

Dreamstime.com: Fiphoto 2cr (room), 16 (room), 19cl (room);
Soleg1974 2cr (boy), 16 (boy), 19cl (boy).

All other images © Dorling Kindersley
For further information see: www.dkimages.com

Printed and bound in China

A WORLD OF IDEAS:
SEE ALL THERE IS TO KNOW

www.dk.com

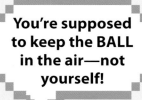

Contents

I love these Scratch books!

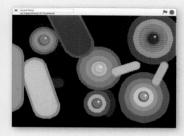

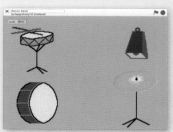

Hello Scratch!

To do any task, a computer needs to follow a list of instructions called a program. In Scratch, it's easy to create programs using ready-made blocks. This book has four fun Scratch projects to do. Can YOU rise to the challenge?

What you'll learn:
• Scratch is easy to learn for beginners
• You need to use **Scratch version 2.0**
• In Scratch, programs are called scripts
• What the ingredients of a Scratch project are

What's what in Scratch

In a typical Scratch project, programs called scripts control characters and objects known as sprites. The sprites appear in a part of the Scratch screen called the stage.

Scratch Cat appears whenever you start a new project. This is a special flying version of him

Sprites

Sprites are things that can move around on the stage in a project. They may be animals, people, shapes, or even spaceships! Scripts bring sprites to life.

Scratch Cat to the rescue!

Scripts

Scripts are made of colored blocks that you drag with a computer mouse and put together like jigsaw pieces. Each block contains one instruction. Scratch reads through a script from top to bottom.

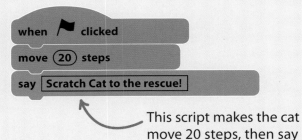

This script makes the cat move 20 steps, then say "Scratch Cat to the rescue!"

READ ME!

This book is based on **Scratch 2.0**, the latest version of Scratch at the time of writing. The games won't work on older versions, so make sure you have 2.0. **See page 40 for details of how to get Scratch**.

Costumes

Many sprites have two or more different pictures, or costumes, they can show on the stage. For example, the sprite "Dinosaur1" has seven costumes. You can see some of them here.

Look! I'm dancing!

The stage

All the action in a Scratch project takes place on the stage. Sprites can move about on the stage, often in front of a background image called a backdrop. Scratch measures distances on the stage in units called steps. The stage is 480 steps wide and 360 steps tall.

The red button stops all scripts

Stage

Backdrop (background picture) helps to create atmosphere

The green flag starts, or runs, the project. It activates all the scripts that you've built

These dinosaurs are all sprites. They switch costumes to dance to music

Each sprite is controlled by its own scripts, which tell it how to move, change size, and more

Right-clicking

Sometimes in Scratch you need to **right-click** with the computer mouse. It's not a problem if your mouse has only one button. Instead of right-clicking, you can usually hold down the control (CTRL/ctrl) or shift key as you click.

Libraries

Scratch has plenty of ready-made items to get you started in its libraries. These are collections of sprites, backdrops, sounds, and music clips that you can use in your own projects.

Video and audio

Webcams and microphones let you interact with sprites. One project in this book uses your computer's webcam, and another uses its microphone. Some websites record your video and audio inputs, but Scratch is safe because it won't record, store, or share them.

A pop-up box always asks permission for a website to use the webcam or microphone

Lights! Camera! Action!

Camera and Microphone Access

cdn.scratch.mit.edu is requesting access to your camera and microphone. If you click Allow, you may be recorded.

✔ Allow   ⊖ Deny

Click **Allow** to give Scratch permission —it won't record you (click **Deny** if you're not sure that a website is safe)

Exploring Scratch

When you open Scratch, this is what you'll see. It's called the Scratch editor, and it has all you need to create your projects. Take some time to explore it.

Experiment!
- Click the buttons and tabs to experiment
- Learn what each block color does
- Try building scripts

Type the name of your project here— this project is a game of Scratch soccer!

Save projects here

Delete sprite or script

Help tool

Click here for full-screen view

Click these to start (run) and stop projects

When you run a Scratch project, you see the action happening on the stage

Click on a sprite on the stage or in the sprite list to select it

All the sprites in your project appear here

You can also select the stage and edit (change) its scripts, backdrops, and sounds

Buttons to add new sprites

Buttons to add new backdrops (background pictures)

A blue box appears around the sprite you have selected. Click on **(i)** for detailed sprite information

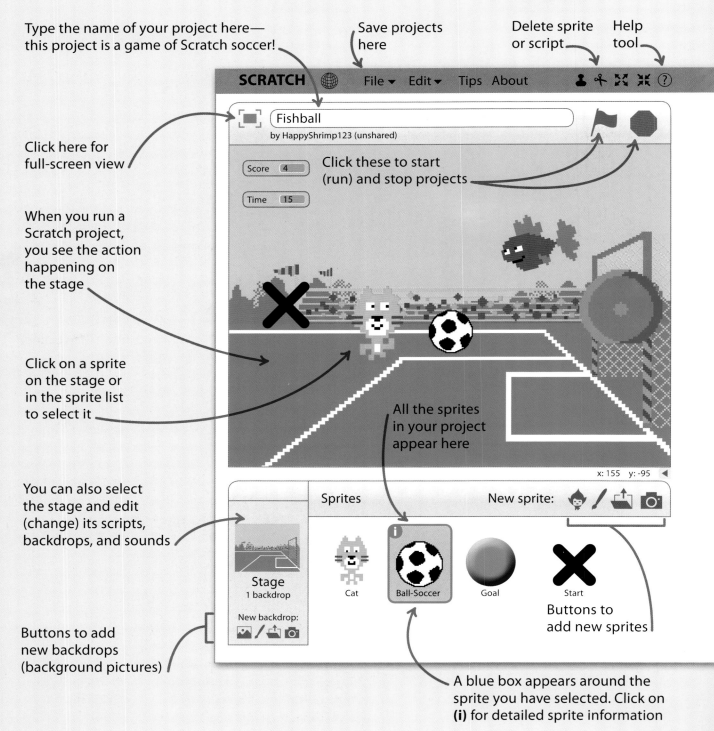

▶ Map of the Scratch editor

The stage is where projects are run. A project's sprites are all shown in the sprite list. Script blocks can be found in the blocks palette. Build your scripts in the scripts area.

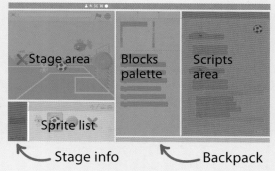

Stage area
Blocks palette
Scripts area
Sprite list

Stage info → ← Backpack

Costumes tab—use this to change a sprite's appearance

Scripts tab

Sounds tab—use this to change the sounds a sprite makes

Click here for step-by-step guides and tips

Saved   [s]   HappyShrimp123 ▼

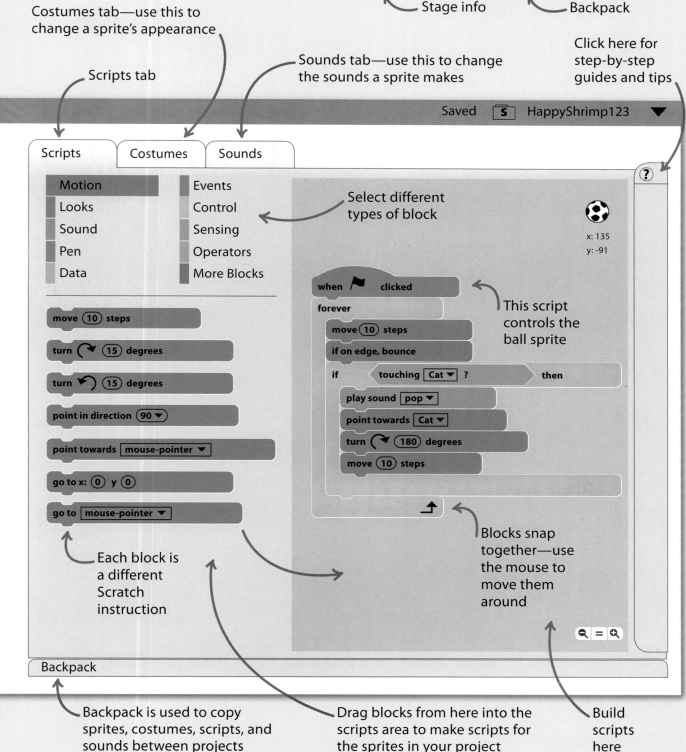

Scripts   Costumes   Sounds

Motion
Looks
Sound
Pen
Data

Events
Control
Sensing
Operators
More Blocks

Select different types of block

x: 135
y: -91

move (10) steps

turn ↻ (15) degrees

turn ↺ (15) degrees

point in direction (90 ▼)

point towards [mouse-pointer ▼]

go to x: (0) y (0)

go to [mouse-pointer ▼]

when ⚑ clicked

forever
  move (10) steps
  if on edge, bounce
  if   touching [Cat ▼] ?   then
    play sound [pop ▼]
    point towards [Cat ▼]
    turn ↻ (180) degrees
    move (10) steps

This script controls the ball sprite

Each block is a different Scratch instruction

Blocks snap together—use the mouse to move them around

Backpack

Backpack is used to copy sprites, costumes, scripts, and sounds between projects

Drag blocks from here into the scripts area to make scripts for the sprites in your project

Build scripts here

Sound Party!

Computer data can be numbers, words, symbols, images, and even sounds. In this project, you'll get some party-loving sprites dancing by inputting musical sounds through your microphone!

What you'll learn:
- That you can use a microphone to make interactive projects
- How to create, control, and delete clones
- How to use Scratch's "ghosting" effect

You can place the balls and buttons anywhere you want

Sprites react to the music

Balls radiate pulses of color that spread out then fade away

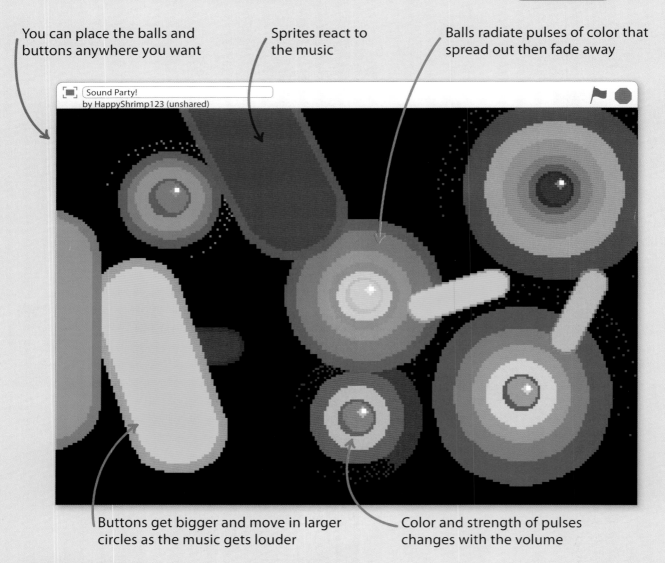

Sound Party!
by HappyShrimp123 (unshared)

Buttons get bigger and move in larger circles as the music gets louder

Color and strength of pulses changes with the volume

▲ What you do

The action on the screen is triggered by the sounds your microphone picks up. Clicking the flag sets the oblong buttons moving in circles. Play some music to start the balls pulsing and make the buttons change size and color. The louder the music, the more on-screen mayhem there is!

Making the backdrop

The moving, pulsing shapes look much better against a dark backdrop than a plain white one. We'll start by using the paint editor to change the backdrop's color.

> **We love a sound party!**

1 Open the Scratch editor: Either choose **Create** on the Scratch website or click the Scratch symbol on your computer. Call your project "Sound Party!" Click on the backdrop in the stage info area, then on the **Backdrops** tab.

Scripts	Backdrops

New backdrop:

1
backdrop1
480x360

Click here to select the backdrop

2 The paint editor will appear to the right of the **Backdrops** tab. Make sure that **Bitmap Mode** is selected in the bottom-right corner.

100%

Bitmap Mode
Convert to vector

Check that **Bitmap Mode** is selected

3 Now select the **Fill with color** tool (the paint pot symbol). Select black or another dark color on the color palette, then click on the drawing area to fill it.

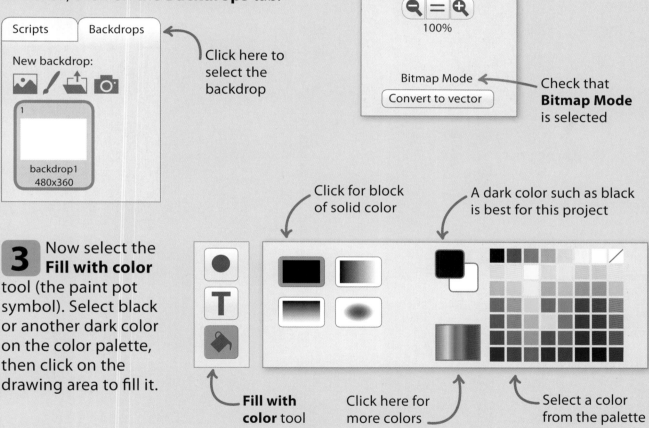

Click for block of solid color

A dark color such as black is best for this project

Fill with color tool

Click here for more colors

Select a color from the palette

4 We don't need the cat for this project. Right-click on the cat with the computer mouse. Choose **delete** from the pop-up menu. Goodbye, Scratch Cat!

> **Oh no! You'll miss the party!**

Cat1

info
duplicate
delete
save to local file
hide

Creating the ball clones

The next task is to make the balls. We'll use clones to produce the pulsing effect. Clones are exact replicas of sprites. They disappear when the game or project ends.

I think you're a clone!

5 Click on the sprite symbol at the top of the sprite list to go to the library. In the library, choose "Ball" and click **OK** to load the sprite into the project. The ball will appear in the sprite list.

Click on the sprite symbol

New sprite:

Choose sprite from library

Ball

6 Use the colored blocks under the **Scripts** tab to build this script for the ball sprite. When music is playing, the script creates 10 clones of the ball sprite every second.

The script inside the **if-then** block runs only if the loudness of the sound input is greater than 0 (a loudness of 0 would be silence).

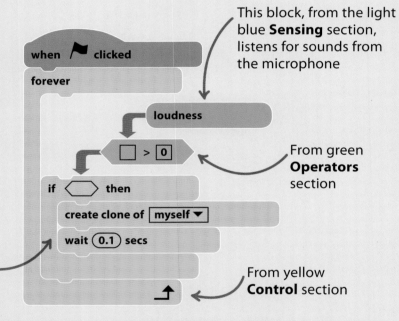

when ⚑ clicked

forever

loudness

☐ > 0

if ⬡ then

create clone of myself ▼

wait 0.1 secs

This block, from the light blue **Sensing** section, listens for sounds from the microphone

From green **Operators** section

From yellow **Control** section

Controlling clones

There are three blocks to use with clones, all found in the yellow **Control** section of the **Scripts** tab.

when I start as a clone

When a clone starts, it runs the script headed with this block.

create clone of myself ▼

This block creates a clone of a sprite. The clone is identical to the sprite and appears in the same position and facing the same direction, so you won't be able to see it until it moves.

delete this clone

This block gets rid of the clone. All clones disappear from the stage when a project stops, leaving just the original sprite.

Ghost effect

The **ghost** effect makes a sprite more transparent (see-through). It's one of seven graphic effects for changing the look of a sprite. To use them, you'll need the purple **change effect by** and **set effect to** blocks. Experiment with the effects to see what each one does.

Select from the drop-down menu

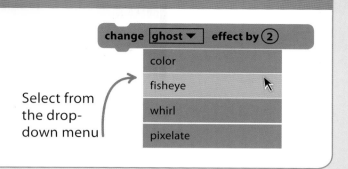

7 Add this second script to the ball to control the clones. It uses blocks from the purple **Looks** section to make each clone change color, grow in size, and fade before vanishing.

repeat loop runs the blocks inside it 50 times, then stops

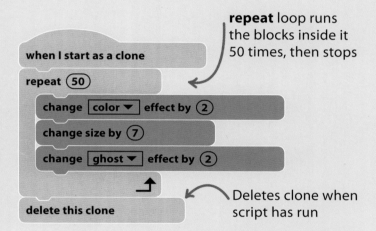

Deletes clone when script has run

8 Play some music, and click the flag to run the project. A pop-up box will appear asking you to let Scratch use your microphone. Select **Allow** (don't worry—for this project, the Scratch website will only detect sound, not record it).

Camera and Microphone Access

cdn.scratch.mit.edu is requesting access to your camera and microphone. If you click Allow, you may be recorded.

✓ Allow   ⊖ Deny

9 Now right-click on the ball sprite and select **duplicate** from the pop-up menu. Do this four times, so that you have five balls in total. Each copy of the ball sprite will have the same code.

Select **duplicate** to copy the ball sprite and its code

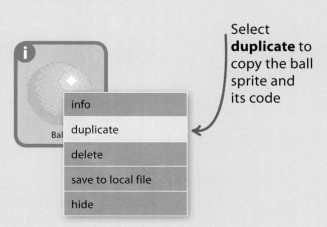

info
duplicate
delete
save to local file
hide

10 The ball has five costumes. Select a different costume for each duplicate.

Give each ball a different costume so that they are all different colors at the start

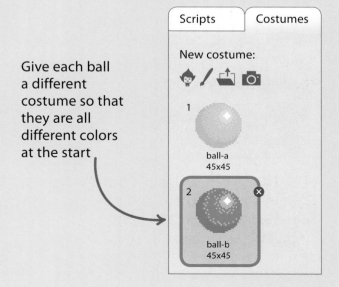

Scripts   Costumes

New costume:

1
ball-a
45x45

2
ball-b
45x45

11 Play a tune and run the project again. Try changing the values of **color**, **size**, and **ghost** in the scripts of the balls, so that each ball responds differently to the music.

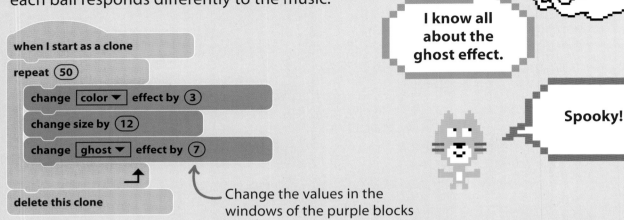

when I start as a clone

repeat 50

change color ▼ effect by 3

change size by 12

change ghost ▼ effect by 7

delete this clone

Change the values in the windows of the purple blocks

> I know all about the ghost effect.

> Spooky!

Bringing in the buttons

It's time to introduce the buttons. The buttons will move in circles when the music plays. They'll also change color and size, depending on the loudness of the music.

12 Load the sprite "Button2" from the library.

Click on the sprite symbol

New sprite: 🎨 / 📤 📷

Choose sprite from library

Button2

Loudness

The **loudness** block reports the volume of sounds detected by your microphone. It gives the volume as a value from 0 to 100.

loudness

You can drop it into the window of another block to make sprites react to sound.

forever

set size to (loudness) %

Check the block's check box to show the volume on the stage.

☑ Loudness

13 Build this script for the button sprite, making sure that you stack the blocks in the correct windows. The script will make the button move in bigger circles as the music gets louder.

Put in left window of **add** block

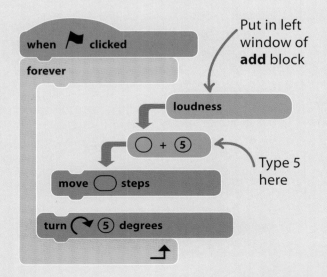

when 🏳 clicked

forever

loudness

○ + 5

move ○ steps

turn ↻ 5 degrees

Type 5 here

Arithmetic operators

Four blocks in the green **Operators** section allow you to do calculations. They are called **arithmetic operators**. You can type numbers into them or use variable blocks. These blocks can also be put inside one another's windows to do more difficult calculations. The inner block is solved first, then the outer block is used.

(7) + (22)
Add (+)

(64) – (28)
Subtract (−)

(11) * (10)
Multiply (×)

(120) / (4)
Divide (÷)

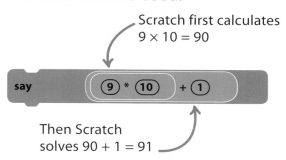

Scratch first calculates
9 × 10 = 90

say ((9) * (10) + (1))

Then Scratch solves 90 + 1 = 91

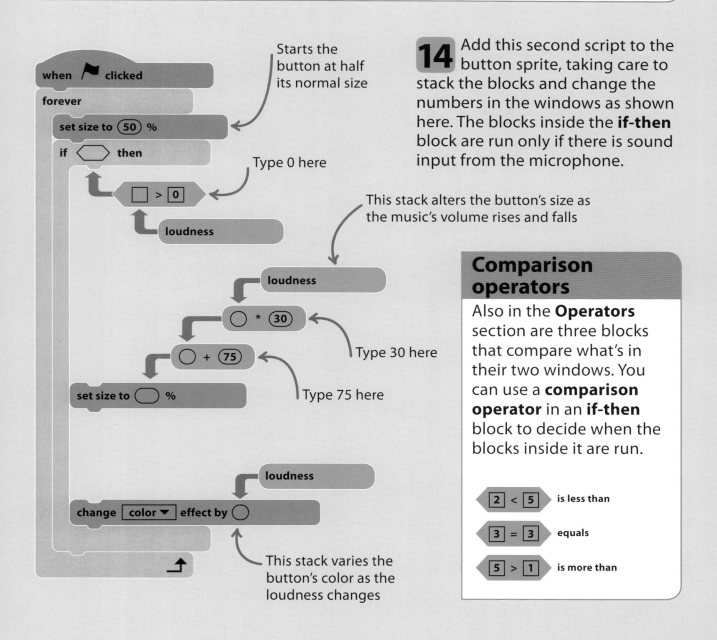

Starts the button at half its normal size

14 Add this second script to the button sprite, taking care to stack the blocks and change the numbers in the windows as shown here. The blocks inside the **if-then** block are run only if there is sound input from the microphone.

when ⚑ clicked

forever

set size to (50) %

if ⬡ then

Type 0 here

□ > 0

loudness

This stack alters the button's size as the music's volume rises and falls

loudness

○ * (30)
Type 30 here

○ + (75)

set size to ○ %
Type 75 here

loudness

change [color ▼] effect by ○

This stack varies the button's color as the loudness changes

Comparison operators

Also in the **Operators** section are three blocks that compare what's in their two windows. You can use a **comparison operator** in an **if-then** block to decide when the blocks inside it are run.

[2] < [5]   **is less than**

[3] = [3]   **equals**

[5] > [1]   **is more than**

15 Duplicate the button sprite five times, so that you end up with six buttons in total. Under the **Costumes** tab, select "button2-b" for three of them and keep the other three as "button2-a."

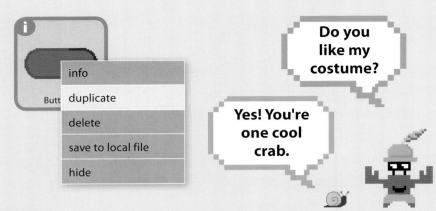

Try changing this value

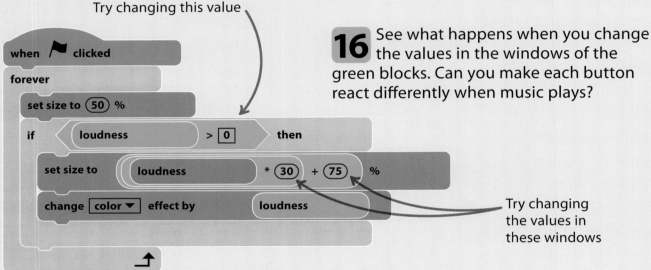

16 See what happens when you change the values in the windows of the green blocks. Can you make each button react differently when music plays?

Try changing the values in these windows

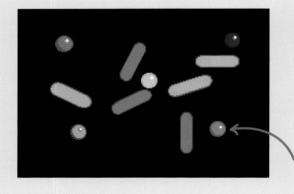

17 The balls and buttons will start from wherever they first appeared on the stage when you created them. If you think the effects would be better if they were in different places, you can move them and they will stay put and start from there!

Position the buttons and balls anywhere you like

Buttons can move over the balls, which lie behind them

18 In Scratch, the last thing you add to the stage will always appear in front of everything else. So the buttons will be in front of the balls. You can change this by altering the order in which you make the balls and buttons.

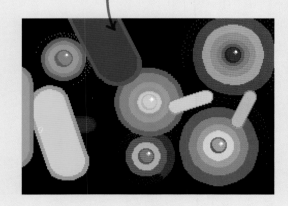

19 Congratulations—you've finished the project! Now let's get this party started!

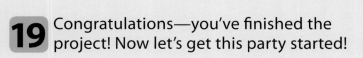

Show what you know
SOUNDS like you've got some tricky problems to deal with here!

1. The _____ block reports the volume of sounds detected by the microphone. The volume has a value between _____ and _____ .

2. This script controls the movement of the buttons. Think about how it works.

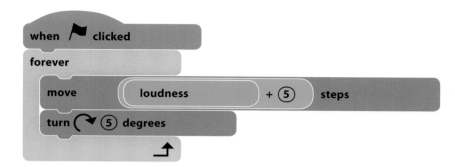

2a. How would you speed up the movement of the buttons?

....

2b. How would you make them turn in smaller circles or go the other way?

....

3. Which number should go in the empty window to make the sprite change size only if there is a very loud noise?

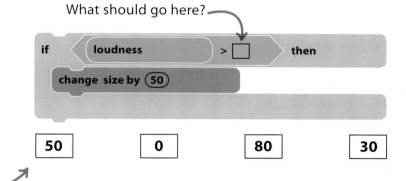

What should go here?

Circle the correct answer

| 50 | 0 | 80 | 30 |

4. Draw lines to link these graphic effects to their correct descriptions.

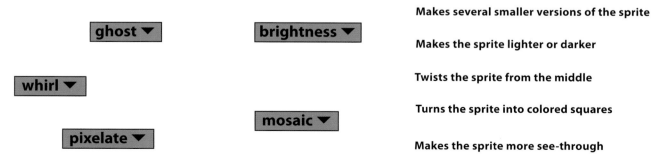

ghost ▼   brightness ▼

Makes several smaller versions of the sprite

Makes the sprite lighter or darker

whirl ▼

Twists the sprite from the middle

Turns the sprite into colored squares

mosaic ▼

pixelate ▼

Makes the sprite more see-through

5. Challenge! Instead of a black backdrop, create a backdrop that changes color to the beat of the music. You'll need to make some code for this.

Keepy-Uppy

In this game, you use your computer's webcam to make yourself the star of the show! Test your reactions as you try to stop the falling soccer ball from hitting the bottom of the stage.

What you'll learn:
• That video can be used to input computer data
• That you can use a webcam to make interactive projects
• How to use Scratch's video blocks in scripts

Your score is shown in the corner of the screen

The ball falls from the top of the screen

You can use any part of your body to hit the ball

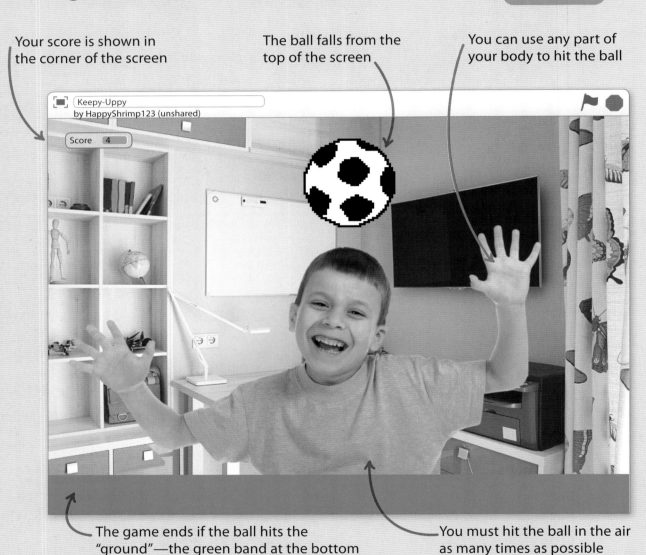

The game ends if the ball hits the "ground"—the green band at the bottom

You must hit the ball in the air as many times as possible

▲ What you do

The ball reacts to movement captured by your webcam. It bounces around the stage as you use your head, hands, arms, feet, legs, or any other body part to keep it in the air. You score a point every time you touch the ball. But watch out—if the ball hits the ground, it's "Game Over!"

Begin with the backdrops

Let's start by making some backdrops. We do this first because we will need to refer to the backdrops in the scripts we build later on.

I can keep this up all day!

Click here to go to backdrop library

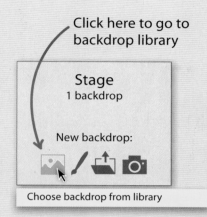

Choose backdrop from library

1 Start a new project and call it "Keepy-Uppy." Right-click on Scratch Cat and select **delete** from the pop-up menu. Go to the stage area and click on **Choose backdrop from library**. In the library, select "blue sky3."

2 Click in the window at the top of the paint editor and type in "Start" to rename the backdrop. Then right-click on the Start backdrop and duplicate it. Call the duplicate "Game Over!"

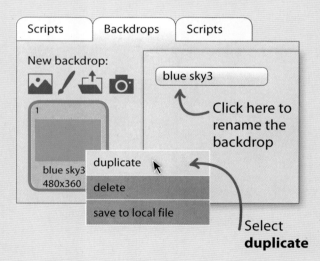

Click here to rename the backdrop

Select **duplicate**

3 With the Game Over! backdrop selected, go to the color palette and choose black. Then select the **Text** (**T**) tool and type out the words "GAME OVER!" in the drawing area.

GAME OVER!

Text tool

Use the corner points to resize the block

Select tool

4 To change the look of the text, click on **Font** at the bottom-left of the paint editor and choose a different font. To resize the text, use the **Select** tool (the arrow symbol) and drag a box around the text. Pull the corner points of the box in or out. When you're happy with the size, click outside the box to stop editing.

GAME OVER!

Ball control!

You can't play Keepy-Uppy without a ball, but we can find one in the sprite library. We'll need to make some scripts for the ball so you can bounce it around the stage.

You won't get past me!

5 In the **Data** section of the **Scripts** tab, make a variable and name it "**Score**." The check box beside it must be checked, so it can be seen on the stage.

A check in this box shows the variable on the stage

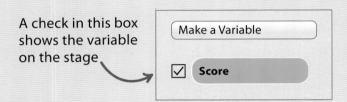

Make a Variable

☑ Score

6 Click on the sprite symbol at the top of the sprite list to go to the library. Select the sprite "Ball-Soccer" and click **OK** to load it into your game.

Click the sprite symbol

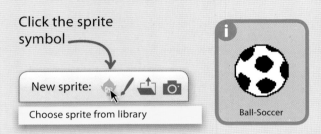

New sprite:
Choose sprite from library

Ball-Soccer

7 We need some sounds for the ball and to announce the end of the game. Go to the **Sounds** tab and click **Choose sound from library** (the speaker symbol). Select "boing" and hit **OK**. Then do the same for "drum bass2."

Scripts | Costumes | Sounds

New sound:
Choose sound from library

Clicking on the speaker takes you to the **Sound Library**

8 Next, assemble these blocks in the ball's scripts area. The script begins the game with the sky-blue backdrop, sets the score to zero, turns on the webcam, and then sets the ball falling.

Makes ball point downward—in Scratch, down is 180, up is 0, right is 90, and left is –90

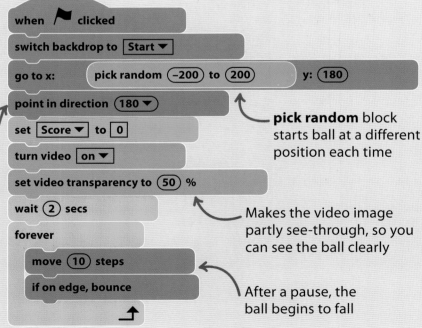

when ⚑ clicked
switch backdrop to Start ▼
go to x: pick random (–200) to (200) y: (180)
point in direction (180 ▼)
set Score ▼ to 0
turn video on ▼
set video transparency to (50) %
wait (2) secs
forever
  move (10) steps
  if on edge, bounce

pick random block starts ball at a different position each time

Makes the video image partly see-through, so you can see the ball clearly

After a pause, the ball begins to fall

9 Now click the flag to test the script. A pop-up box will ask permission for Scratch to use your webcam. You'll need to click **Allow** for the script to run (don't worry, you won't be recorded).

10 You should be able to see yourself on the screen with the ball bouncing up and down. If you can't, check that there are no mistakes in your script.

Video blocks

As well as the **turn video on/off** block, there are two other useful video blocks.

Number range is 0–100

set video transparency to (50) %

High numbers make the video image more transparent (see-through). Lower numbers make it less transparent.

Click here to select **this sprite** or **Stage**

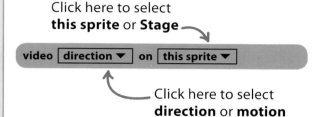

video [direction ▼] on [this sprite ▼]

Click here to select **direction** or **motion**

This block senses how much motion there is in the video image or what the direction of motion is, either in relation to a selected sprite or over the whole stage.

Coordinates

Scratch uses a pair of numbers called x–y coordinates to pinpoint a sprite's position on the stage. The x coordinate tells you where the sprite is across the stage, left or right. The y coordinate shows its up or down position. Coordinates get bigger the farther right or up you go, and get smaller the farther left or down you go. Keepy-Uppy uses coordinates to start the ball at the top of the stage in a random left–right position.

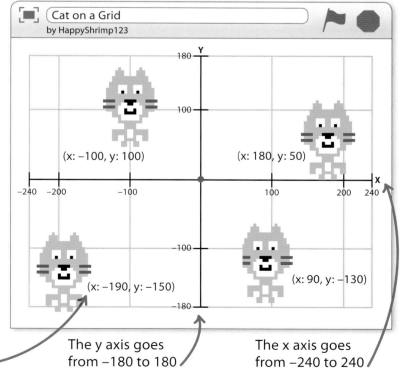

Cat on a Grid
by HappyShrimp123

(x: –100, y: 100)

(x: 180, y: 50)

(x: –190, y: –150)

(x: 90, y: –130)

The x coordinate is always written first

The y axis goes from –180 to 180

The x axis goes from –240 to 240

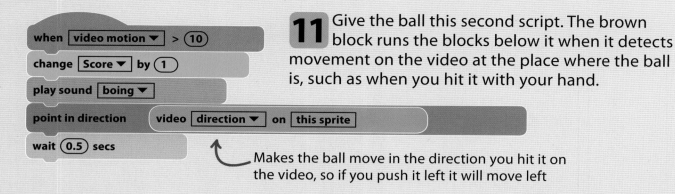

11 Give the ball this second script. The brown block runs the blocks below it when it detects movement on the video at the place where the ball is, such as when you hit it with your hand.

Makes the ball move in the direction you hit it on the video, so if you push it left it will move left

12 Now let's make another sprite. Click on **Paint new sprite** (the paintbrush) at the top of the sprite list to open the paint editor. Choose a grass-green color and use the **Rectangle** tool to draw a thick line across the bottom of the drawing area. Select the sprite in the sprite list, click on the blue (i) in its top corner, and rename it "Ground."

Click here

Rectangle tool

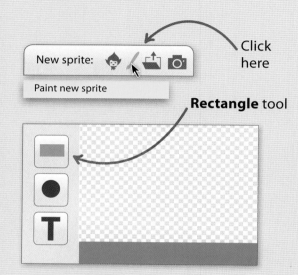

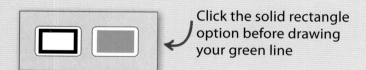

Click the solid rectangle option before drawing your green line

13 Add this final script to the ball sprite. It ends the game and turns off the webcam if the ball touches the ground (the green band at the bottom of the stage). Click the flag to test the game. If there are problems, check that the blocks in each script are in the correct order.

14 That's it—you've finished building Keepy-Uppy. Challenge your friends to see who can keep the ball in the air the longest and score the most points!

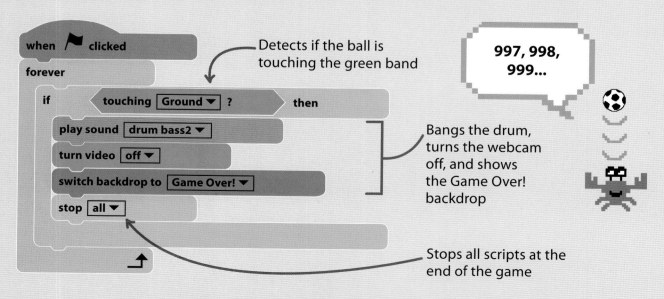

Detects if the ball is touching the green band

997, 998, 999...

Bangs the drum, turns the webcam off, and shows the Game Over! backdrop

Stops all scripts at the end of the game

Show what you know
Are your Scratch skills as good as your ball skills? Test yourself!

1. Circle the correct answers.

1a. The **turn video on** / **start camera** block switches on the webcam.

1b. We can use the webcam as **input** / **output** for a Scratch program.

1c. The **turn video off** / **stop camera** block switches off the video.

2. These blocks control the movement of the ball sprite. What happens if you change the code from **Move 10 steps** to:

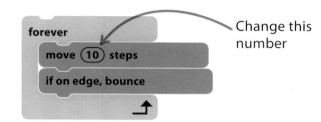

Change this number

2a. Move 30 steps ....

2b. Move 1 steps ....

2c. Move 0 steps ....

3. Read each sentence and check the correct box.   **True**   **False**

3a. The score goes up by 2 points if you head the ball.   ☐   ☐

3b. When you hit the ball, a "boing" sound is played.   ☐   ☐

3c. The game ends if you touch the ball with your hand.   ☐   ☐

4. If you deleted the script you made in Step 13, would the game still work?

....

....

Change this number to 30

```
when  video motion ▼  > (10)
change  Score ▼  by (1)
play sound  boing ▼
point in direction    video  direction ▼  on  this sprite
wait (0.5) secs
```

5. This is the script from Step 11. If you change the **when video motion** block to **> 30**, does it make the game easier or harder?

....

6. Challenge! Add a timer and some new code so that your total score is now the number of keepy-ups + the number of seconds you lasted.

Monkey Rescue

Scrolling is sliding sprites together in the same direction so that a character appears to move through a scene. In Monkey Rescue, scrolling will make the cat fly across the city saving monkeys!

What you'll learn:
• How to make sprites scroll across the stage
• That sprites can send messages to each other
• How to make sprites appear and vanish at certain points in a game

The counters show the numbers of lives left and monkeys rescued

Starry night background

The stranded monkeys are stuck on top of tall buildings

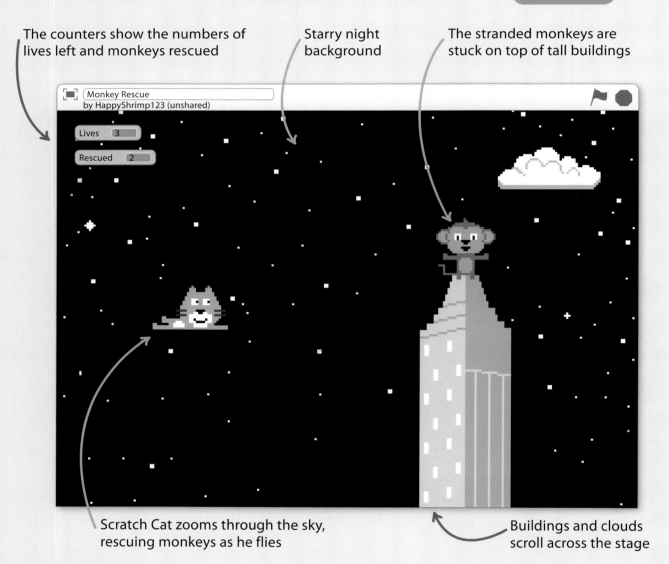

Scratch Cat zooms through the sky, rescuing monkeys as he flies

Buildings and clouds scroll across the stage

▲ What you do

Press the space bar and Scratch Cat rises in the air—do nothing and he falls downward. When Scratch Cat touches a monkey, he rescues it and it vanishes. You have five lives. Hit a building or a cloud and you lose a life. How many monkeys can you save before all your lives are gone?

Superhero Scratch Cat!

For Monkey Rescue, we'll use a flying version of Scratch Cat instead of the normal cat sprite. Let's set the scene and get him flying through the night sky over Scratch City.

I'm the big hero in this game!

1 Start a new project and call it "Monkey Rescue." Delete the normal Scratch Cat. Go to the **Sprite Library**, select "Cat1 Flying," and hit **OK** to load it.

Click the sprite symbol

Choose sprite from library

Cat1 Flying

2 Now add some sounds. Under the **Sounds** tab, click on **Choose sound from library** (the speaker). In the library, select "chee chee" and click **OK**. Do the same for "meow2."

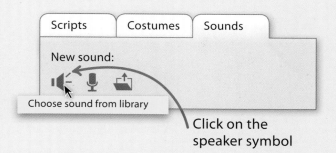

Choose sound from library

Click on the speaker symbol

3 Next, build this code in Flying Scratch's scripts area. The x–y numbers, or coordinates, tell the cat where to appear on the stage at the start. The **forever** loop causes him to drop continually. Click the flag to test the script.

Cat will appear in front of everything else on the stage

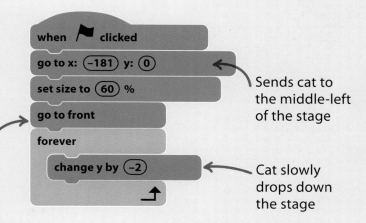

Sends cat to the middle-left of the stage

Cat slowly drops down the stage

4 Give Flying Scratch this second script. It allows you to control the cat's upward movement. Every time you press the space bar, he will move up 20 steps.

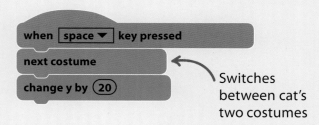

Switches between cat's two costumes

5 Go to the stage info area, at the bottom-left of the Scratch editor. Click on the **Choose backdrop from library** symbol. Select "stars" in the library and hit **OK**.

Click here for the **Backdrop Library**

New backdrop:

Choose backdrop from library

Scrolling sprites

Now that we've set the scene, let's add three more things: the buildings, the clouds that drift by overhead, and the poor, stranded monkeys.

7 Add this script to the Buildings sprite. The sprite will scroll across the stage from right to left. There are 10 costumes. The purple block picks a random costume for each pass across the stage.

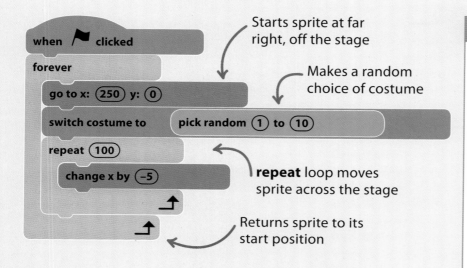

Starts sprite at far right, off the stage

Makes a random choice of costume

repeat loop moves sprite across the stage

Returns sprite to its start position

8 Now go back to the sprite list, click on the sprite symbol, and choose "Cloud." Load the sprite into the game.

Cloud

9 Put these blocks together for the cloud. It starts the cloud near the top of the stage but off to the right, then moves it across, from right to left.

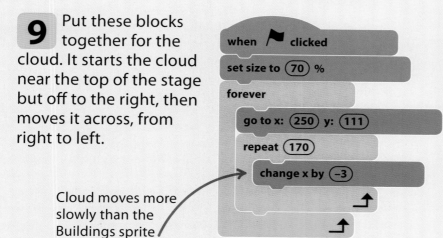

Cloud moves more slowly than the Buildings sprite

6 Click on the sprite symbol at the top of the sprite list to go to the library. Choose the sprite "Buildings" and click **OK** to load it into your game.

Click for the **Sprite Library**

New sprite:

Choose sprite from library

Buildings

Scrolling

Although you see the cat fly through the city, he doesn't actually move forward. Instead, the buildings, clouds, and monkeys scroll (slide across the stage) in the direction opposite to the way he's facing. This creates the illusion that he's flying toward them. By randomly switching the Buildings sprite's costumes, the code makes it looks as if the cat is moving through a changing city scene.

10 Return to the sprite list and load the final sprite, "Monkey2," from the **Sprite Library**.

Monkey2

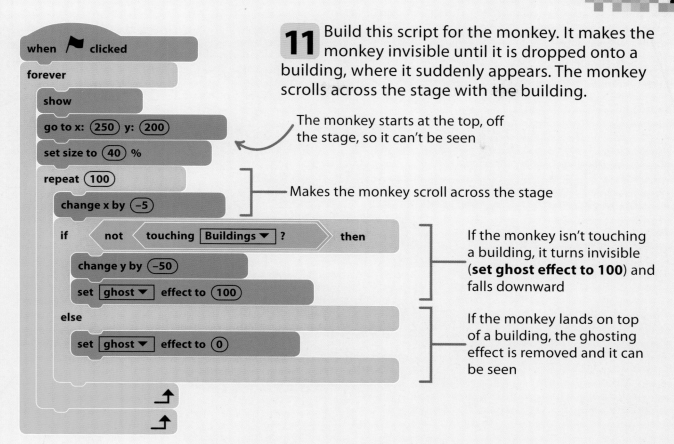

11 Build this script for the monkey. It makes the monkey invisible until it is dropped onto a building, where it suddenly appears. The monkey scrolls across the stage with the building.

The monkey starts at the top, off the stage, so it can't be seen

Makes the monkey scroll across the stage

If the monkey isn't touching a building, it turns invisible (**set ghost effect to 100**) and falls downward

If the monkey lands on top of a building, the ghosting effect is removed and it can be seen

Even superheroes need scripts!

The next task is to make some scripts for the cat to set up a scoring system and the number of lives he has before the game ends.

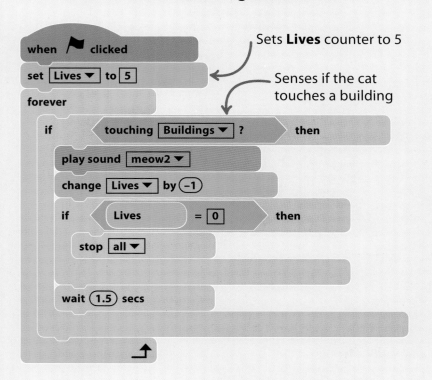

Sets **Lives** counter to 5

Senses if the cat touches a building

12 Make two variables called "**Lives**" and "**Rescued**." Make sure their check boxes are checked so they show on the stage.

These must be checked

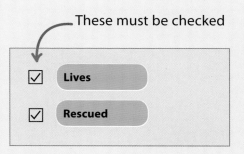

13 Select the cat and give it this script. It sets the cat's **Lives** counter on the stage to 5. When the cat touches a building, a "meow" sound plays and a life is lost. When there are no lives left (**Lives = 0**), all scripts stop running and the game ends.

Messages

Scratch sprites can broadcast (send out) messages to "talk" to each other.

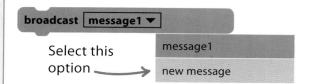

Select this option → message1 / new message

This block sends out a message telling other sprites to do something. Click the arrow to create a new instruction.

This block tells other sprites to do something, such as vanish. It waits until they finish before continuing.

when I receive Vanish ▼

This block runs any script below it when it receives a message, such as **Vanish**.

14 Duplicate the cat's script from Step 13, but delete the **set Lives to 5** block. Select **Cloud** in the **touching?** block. Now the cat will also lose a life if he touches a cloud.

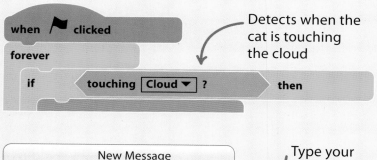

Detects when the cat is touching the cloud

15 Using a brown **broadcast** block, select **new message** from its drop-down menu. Type "**Vanish**" into the pop-up box.

Type your message in here

16 Build this new script for the cat. If the cat touches the monkey, the "chee chee" sound plays, the **Rescued** score goes up by 1, and the monkey is sent the message **Vanish**.

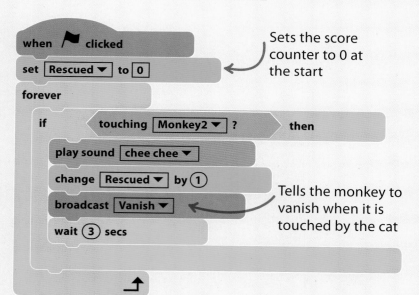

Sets the score counter to 0 at the start

Tells the monkey to vanish when it is touched by the cat

17 Create this final script for the monkey. When the monkey gets the message **Vanish**, it disappears. All done! Have fun helping Scratch Cat rescue those monkeys!

This block runs any script below it when it receives the message vanish →

Show what you know
Will you fly through this quiz… or will you need rescuing?

1. Circle the correct answers.

Press the space bar and the cat moves **up / down**. This means the sprite's

x coordinate / y coordinate value will have **increased / decreased**.

2. Lives is set to 5. What's the value of **Lives** if these blocks are run?

2a. change [Lives ▼] by (-1)   Value of lives is now..............

2b. change [Lives ▼] by (5)   Value of lives is now..............

2c. change [Lives ▼] by (1) - (2)   Value of lives is now..............

3. What would happen if the Buildings sprite's script used the **next**

costume block instead of **switch costume to pick random 1 to 10**?

switch costume to   pick random (1) to (10)   ✗   next costume   ✓

....

4. If a sprite starts at position (50, 50), where
will it be after these blocks of code are run?

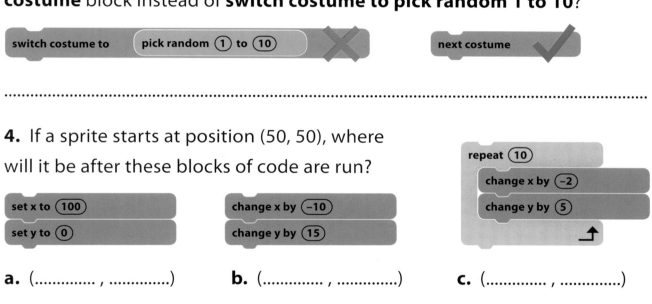

set x to (100)
set y to (0)

change x by (-10)
change y by (15)

repeat (10)
change x by (-2)
change y by (5)

a. (.............. , ...)   **b.** (.............. , ...)   **c.** (.............. , ...)

5. Making Flying Scratch change costumes all the time probably makes the
game harder. How could you solve this problem?

....

6. The Buildings sprite's costume "building-h" is so high it's very difficult
to rescue the monkey. What change might fix this?

....

7. Challenge! Change the cloud's code to make the clouds move more
quickly across the stage every time you rescue a monkey.

Memory Master

Put your memory to the test with this mind-bending musical game! What is the longest sequence of sounds you can remember? Compete with your friends to see who's the Memory Master!

The number of sounds goes up by one with each level, so **Level 7** has seven sounds to remember

Scratch plays a sequence of sounds on these instruments

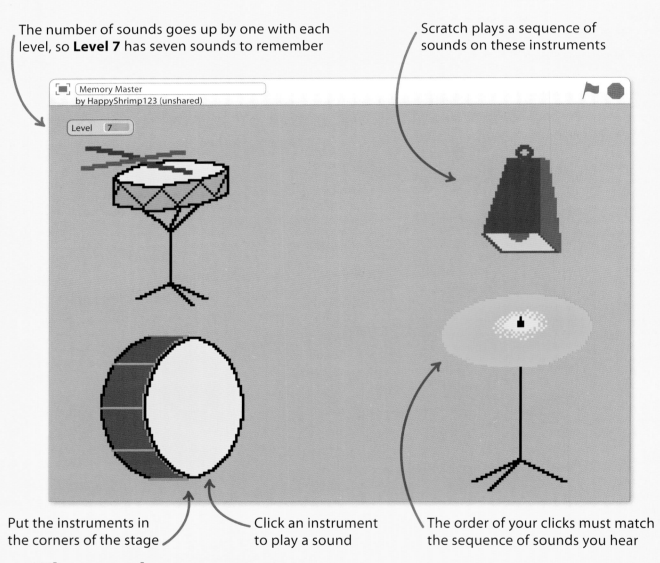

Put the instruments in the corners of the stage

Click an instrument to play a sound

The order of your clicks must match the sequence of sounds you hear

▲ What you do

When you click the flag, you will hear a sequence of sounds played on the instruments. Listen carefully, then click the instruments to repeat the order correctly and progress to the next level. Be on your guard—the sequence gets longer each time, and a single mistake ends the game!

Instructions and backdrops

To begin, we'll add a nice backdrop for the instruments, create a "Game Over!" backdrop for the end of the game, and make an instructions sprite to tell players what to do.

1 Start a new project and call it "Memory Master." Delete Scratch Cat, then go to the stage info area, and load "purple" from the **Backdrop Library**. Rename it "Start."

2 Next, duplicate the Start backdrop and rename it "Game Over!" Use the **Text** tool (**T**) in the paint editor to type "GAME OVER!" onto the backdrop. Change the font or resize the text with the **Select** tool if you need to. This is the same as what you did in Steps 2–4 of Keepy-Uppy (see page 17).

3 Now go to the sprite list and click on the paintbrush symbol to create a new sprite. Call it "Instructions." In the paint editor, choose black from the palette, select the **Text** tool (**T**), and type out the instructions exactly as shown on the right.

4 Use the **Select** tool to move the text so it appears in the middle of the stage (the instruments will be in the four corners). You can resize it later if necessary.

5 Add this script to the Instructions sprite. When the flag is clicked, it will show the instructions on the stage at the start of the game. When you press the space bar, the instructions will disappear.

Dig my crazy rhythm!

Use the corner points to resize the text

Select tool

GAME OVER!

Listen to the sounds. Click the instruments to repeat the sounds in the correct order.

The sequence starts with one sound, but it gets longer each time. Make a mistake and it's "Game Over!"

Press the space bar to start the game.

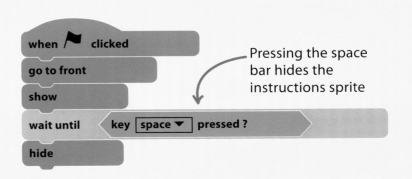

Pressing the space bar hides the instructions sprite

when ⚑ clicked
go to front
show
wait until key space ▼ pressed ?
hide

Lists help us remember!

Next, we need to make some variables, and also a list. The list will keep a record of the number and order of sounds that the instruments play.

Um, what did I want at the store?

You should have made a list!

☐	**Checker**
☐	**Counter**
☑	**Level**
☐	**Random**

Only check this box

6 Under the **Data** tab, select **Make a variable**. Type "**Checker**" as the variable's name and click **OK**. Make three more variables. Call them "**Counter**," "**Level**," and "**Random**." All of their check boxes should be left unchecked, except for the one next to **Level**.

7 Below the **Make a Variable** button under the **Data** tab, you'll see another button called **Make a List**. Select that and type "**Sound list**" in the pop-up box's window. Click **OK**. When it appears under the **Data** blocks, uncheck its check box.

New List

List name: | Sound list

● For all sprites ○ For this sprite only

OK | Cancel

Lists

Making a list is a great way to store a set of information, such as numbers or words. Lots of programming languages use lists. They are handy for all sorts of things, from creating leaderboards and doing complex calculations to giving sprites artificial intelligence, so they look like they make their own decisions. In Memory Master, we use a list to store the sounds made by our musical instruments.

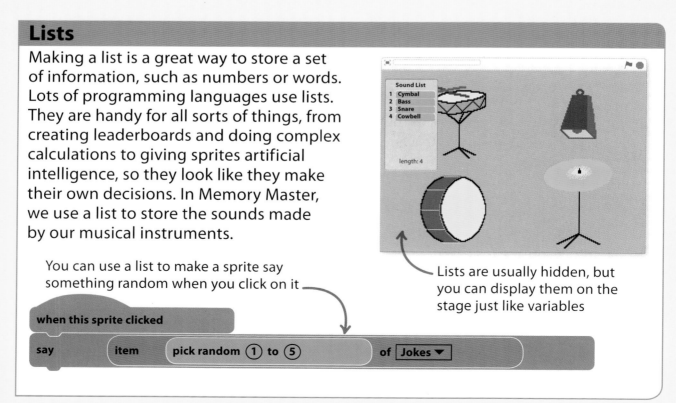

Sound List
1 Cymbal
2 Bass
3 Snare
4 Cowbell

length: 4

Lists are usually hidden, but you can display them on the stage just like variables

You can use a list to make a sprite say something random when you click on it

when this sprite clicked

say | item | pick random ① to ⑤ | of | Jokes ▼

Adding the instruments

There are four instruments in the Scratch percussion orchestra, so lets load them into the project and give them some scripts.

8 First, load the big bass drum ("Drum-Bass") from the **Sprite Library**. It has three sounds.

Drum-Bass

9 Now give the Drum-Bass sprite this script. When the player clicks on the drum, **Checker** reports if it matches the correct sound stored at that position in the list. If it does, the bass drum sound plays and the **Checker** increases by 1 (so the next sound it checks will be one place further on in the list). If the player clicks the wrong instrument, the game ends. You can see a similar script for the Cymbal in full at Step 13 on page 32.

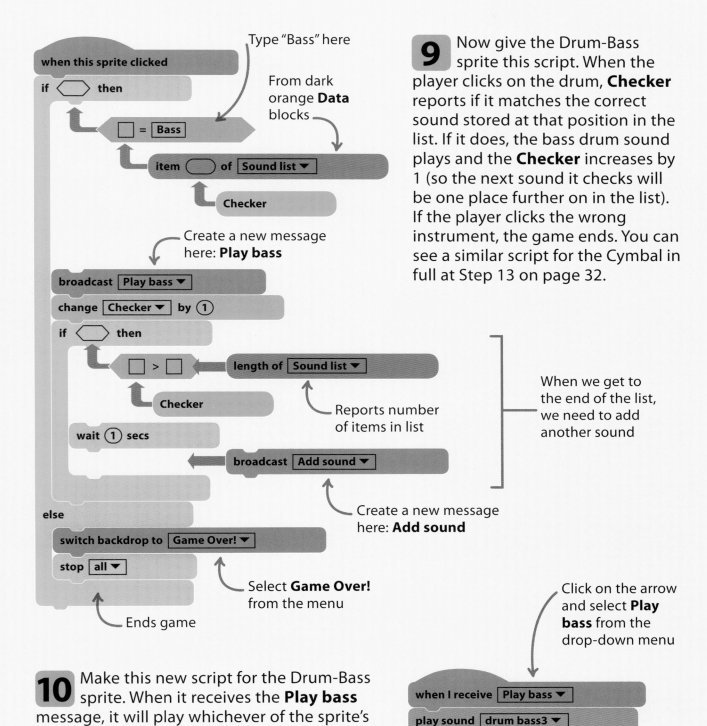

Type "Bass" here

From dark orange **Data** blocks

```
when this sprite clicked
if <      > then
        <   = Bass   >
                item (   ) of Sound list ▼
                        Checker
```

Create a new message here: **Play bass**

```
    broadcast Play bass ▼
    change Checker ▼ by (1)
    if <      > then
            <   >   <   length of Sound list ▼
                    Checker
        wait (1) secs
                broadcast Add sound ▼
    else
        switch backdrop to Game Over! ▼
    stop all ▼
```

Reports number of items in list

When we get to the end of the list, we need to add another sound

Create a new message here: **Add sound**

Select **Game Over!** from the menu

Ends game

10 Make this new script for the Drum-Bass sprite. When it receives the **Play bass** message, it will play whichever of the sprite's sounds you have selected in the window of the **play sound** block.

Click on the arrow and select **Play bass** from the drop-down menu

```
when I receive Play bass ▼
play sound drum bass3 ▼
```

Choose the drum sound you like best. Click on the pink block to hear sound

11 Now load these three new sprites from the **Sprite Library**: "Cymbal," "Cowbell," and "Drum-Snare." Put the four instruments in the corners of the stage.

Cymbal

Cowbell

Drum-Snare

12 Add the same scripts you built for the Drum-Bass sprite to each of the new sprites. The easiest way is to click, drag, and drop the scripts from one sprite onto another. This will copy the scripts to the new sprite.

Sprites   New sprite:

Drum-Bass

when I receive [Play bass ▼]
play sound [drum bass3 ▼]

Release the mouse when the pointer is over the sprite you want to copy the code to

13 Create a new message for each instrument sprite. For example, for the cymbal click on the **broadcast** block's arrow and select **new message**. Type "**Play cymbal**" into the pop-up window and click **OK**. Also change "Bass" to "Cymbal" in the window of the green **add** block.

Change the name here to "Cymbal." Use "Cowbell" and "Snare" for the other two instruments

when this sprite clicked

if < item (Checker) of [Sound list ▼] = [Cymbal] > then

    broadcast [Play cymbal ▼]

    change [Checker ▼] by (1)

    if < Checker > length of [Sound list ▼] > then

        wait (1) secs

        broadcast [Add sound ▼]

else

    switch backdrop to [Game Over! ▼]

    stop [all ▼]

Add a new message for each instrument sprite

14 For each instrument, select the correct message in the window of the **when I receive** block, and choose a sound in the **play sound** block.

Select the correct message here

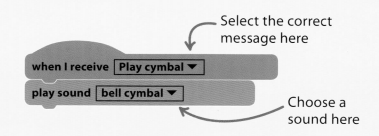

when I receive [Play cymbal ▼]
play sound [bell cymbal ▼]

Choose a sound here

Scripting the list

In the stage's scripts area, we'll build the code for creating the list, playing it back, and clearing it before each new game.

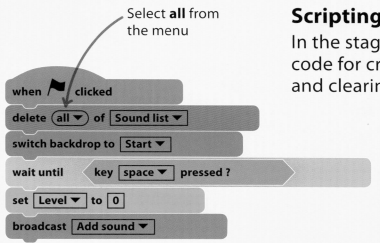

Select **all** from the menu

```
when 🏴 clicked
delete (all ▼) of [Sound list ▼]
switch backdrop to [Start ▼]
wait until    key [space ▼] pressed ?
set [Level ▼] to (0)
broadcast [Add sound ▼]
```

15 Click on the stage info area and add this script. Clicking the flag clears the information stored in the list from the last game. Pressing the space bar starts a new game.

16 Add this code to the stage. It numbers the instrument sounds from 1 to 4. When it receives the **Add sound** message, it picks a random number from 1 to 4 and adds that sound to the list of sounds to be played. Then it broadcasts the message **Play sound list**, which you'll have to create in a **broadcast** block.

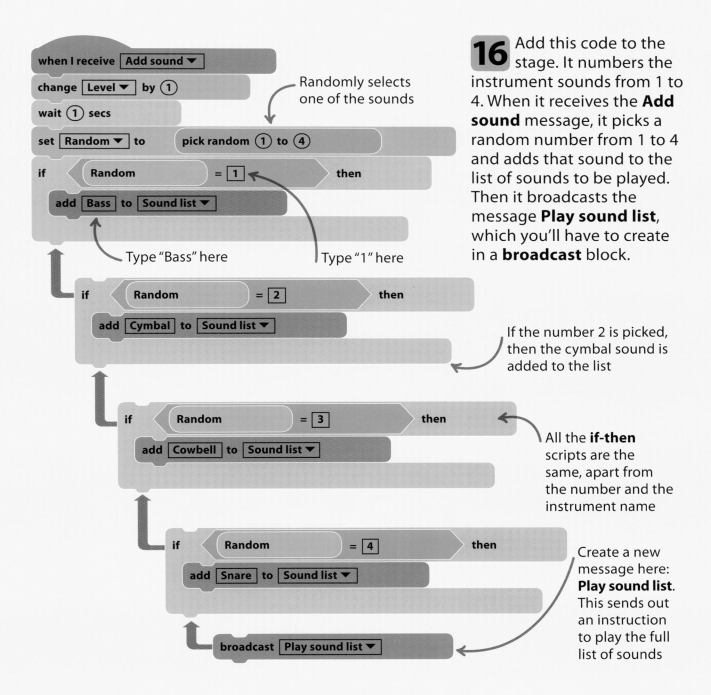

Randomly selects one of the sounds

Type "Bass" here

Type "1" here

If the number 2 is picked, then the cymbal sound is added to the list

All the **if-then** scripts are the same, apart from the number and the instrument name

Create a new message here: **Play sound list**. This sends out an instruction to play the full list of sounds

17 Now give the stage this third and final script. When it receives the **Play sound list** message, the script uses the **Counter** variable to play all the sounds in the order they were added to the list.

Click and select message

Counter keeps track as the script works down the list, starting with the first sound

List stops playing when the value of the variable **Counter** is greater than number of sounds in the list

Script plays whichever sound is first in the list

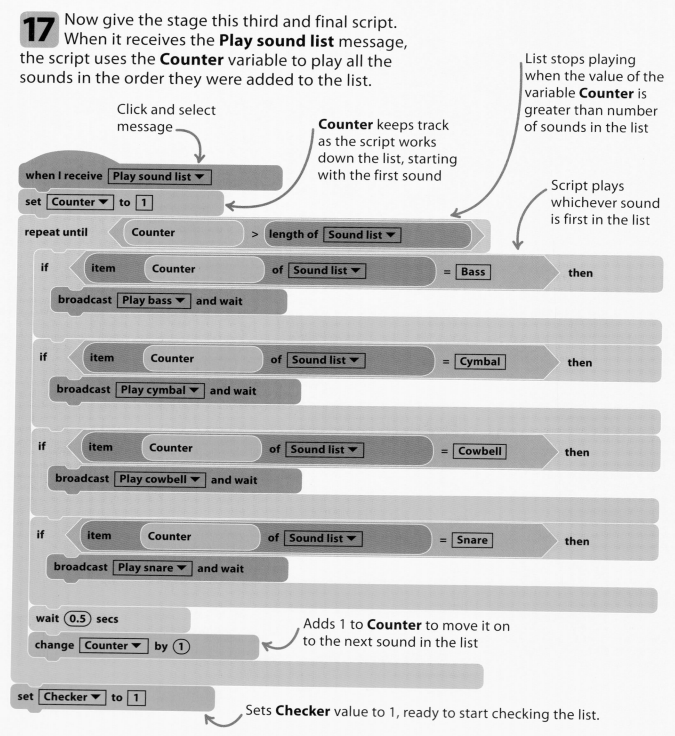

```
when I receive [Play sound list ▼]
set [Counter ▼] to [1]
repeat until ⟨ (Counter) > (length of [Sound list ▼]) ⟩
    if ⟨ (item (Counter) of [Sound list ▼]) = [Bass] ⟩ then
        broadcast [Play bass ▼] and wait
    if ⟨ (item (Counter) of [Sound list ▼]) = [Cymbal] ⟩ then
        broadcast [Play cymbal ▼] and wait
    if ⟨ (item (Counter) of [Sound list ▼]) = [Cowbell] ⟩ then
        broadcast [Play cowbell ▼] and wait
    if ⟨ (item (Counter) of [Sound list ▼]) = [Snare] ⟩ then
        broadcast [Play snare ▼] and wait
    wait (0.5) secs
    change [Counter ▼] by (1)
set [Checker ▼] to [1]
```

Adds 1 to **Counter** to move it on to the next sound in the list

Sets **Checker** value to 1, ready to start checking the list.

18 Run the project. The code is complicated, so check that the project's working as it should. If something's not right, look closely at every script to make sure there are no mistakes. You may want to resize the text and move the instruments so that the instructions are easy to read. When everything's OK, start playing!

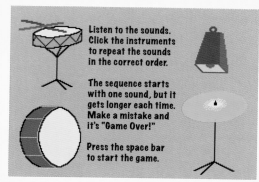

Listen to the sounds. Click the instruments to repeat the sounds in the correct order.

The sequence starts with one sound, but it gets longer each time. Make a mistake and it's "Game Over!"

Press the space bar to start the game.

Show what you know
Are you a Scratch Master as well as a Memory Master? Find out!

1. Circle the correct answers.

1a. The **counter / checker** variable is used when the program plays through the sequence of sounds in the list.

1b. The **counter / checker** variable is used when the player clicks an instrument.

2. The check box next to **Sound list** under the **Data** tab is unchecked. Why is this necessary?

....

....

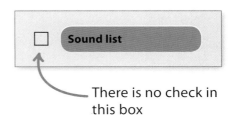

There is no check in this box

3. Draw lines to link these list blocks to their correct descriptions.

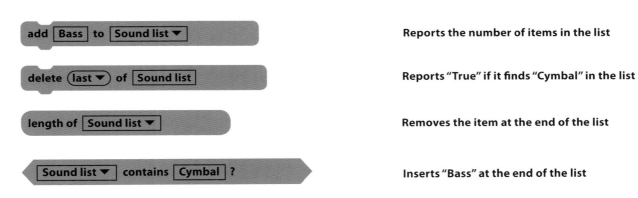

Reports the number of items in the list

Reports "True" if it finds "Cymbal" in the list

Removes the item at the end of the list

Inserts "Bass" at the end of the list

4. Bug hunt! There are three mistakes, or bugs, in this script for the stage. Can you find them? Circle the errors.

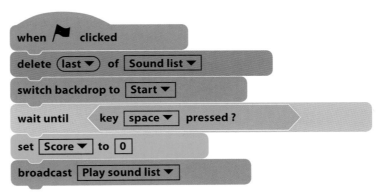

5. Challenge! Make Memory Master even more challenging by adding an extra instrument, the "Drum-Tabla," to the game. Change the scripts to handle five instruments.

Load this sprite from the library

Drum-Tabla

Solutions

You've risen to the challenge and completed every task set before you! Time to check your "Show what you know" answers. How did you do?

Let's give them the answers!

pages 8–15 Sound Party!

1. The **loudness** block reports the volume of sounds detected by the microphone. The volume has a value between **0** and **100**.

2a. To speed up the buttons, increase the number of steps in the **move** block. For example, change it to **loudness + 10**.

2b. To make the buttons' circles smaller, increase the number of degrees in the **turn** block. To make them go the other way, swap the clockwise ↻ **turn** block for the counterclockwise ↺ **turn** block in the **Motion** section.

3. To make the sprite change size only if there is a very loud noise, **80** should go in the window. (Remember: 100 is the loudest volume.)

4.

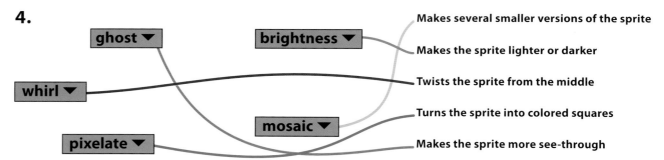

		Makes several smaller versions of the sprite
ghost ▼	brightness ▼	Makes the sprite lighter or darker
whirl ▼		Twists the sprite from the middle
	mosaic ▼	Turns the sprite into colored squares
pixelate ▼		Makes the sprite more see-through

5. Challenge! First, you'll need to change the black backdrop back to white in the paint editor. Then give it a script like this.

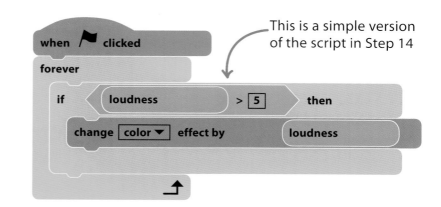

This is a simple version of the script in Step 14

when ⚑ clicked
forever
  if ⟨ loudness > 5 ⟩ then
    change [color ▼] effect by loudness

pages 16–21 Keepy-Uppy

1a. The **turn video on** / **start camera** block switches on the webcam.

2b. We can use the webcam as **input** / **output** for a Scratch program.

3c. The **turn video off** / **stop camera** block switches off the video.

2a. Move 30 steps makes the ball move more quickly.

2b. Move 1 steps makes the ball move more slowly.

2c. Move 0 steps stops the ball from moving at all.

3a. False. The score will go up by only 1 point.

3b. True.

3c. False. Any movement can count as hitting the ball—the game can't tell whether it's a hand, foot, or head that makes contact with the ball.

4. The script in Step 13 stops the game when the ball hits the ground. If you remove it, the game will still work and you'll be able to keep hitting the ball even after it has touched the ground.

5. When you change the **when video motion** block to **> 30**, you have to move your body more to hit the ball. This makes the game harder.

6. Challenge! Add these two scripts to the ball. The **timer** block is built into Scratch. It counts the seconds since the program started. We need a new variable, called "**Total Score**," to hold the combined score.

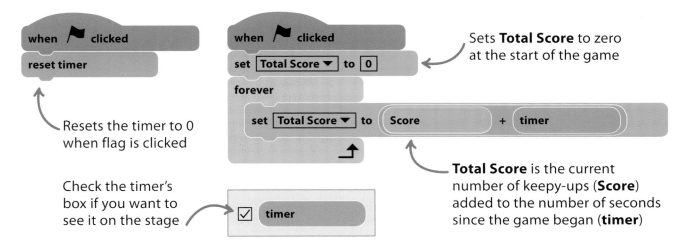

1. Press the space bar and the cat moves (up)/ down. This means the sprite's **x coordinate /(y coordinate)** value will have (increased)/ decreased.

2a. The value of **Lives** is now 4, since 5 – 1 = 4.

2b. The value of **Lives** is now 10, since 5 + 5 = 10.

2c. The value of **Lives** is now 4, since 1 – 2 = –1, and 5 – 1 = 4.

3. The costumes would change in the order they appear under the **Costumes** tab. This would make the game easier, because you would know when each building was going to scroll across the stage.

4a. (100 , 0) **4b.** (40 , 65) **4c.** (30 , 100)

Remember: The x coordinate is written first and then the y coordinate.

5. Remove the **next costume** block from Step 4. Use the cat's horizontal costume, which glides more easily between the clouds and buildings.

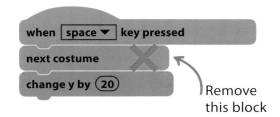

Remove this block

6. Delete the "building-h" costume and change Step 7's **pick random** range to **1 to 9**. Alternatively, make the y value in Step 7's **go to x–y** block a minus number, such as **–40**, so the sprite starts lower down on the stage.

7. Challenge! Make this change to the cloud's **change x by** block. At the start, **Rescued = 0** and the clouds move left in 3-step jumps. Saving a monkey adds an extra step to each jump, making the clouds speed up.

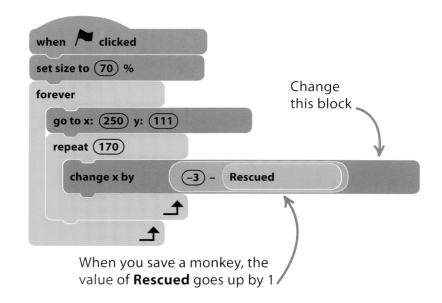

Change this block

When you save a monkey, the value of **Rescued** goes up by 1

1a. The ⟨counter⟩/ **checker** variable is used when the program plays through the sequence of sounds in the list.

1b. The **counter** /⟨checker⟩ variable is used when the player clicks an instrument.

2. The check box of the **Sound list** is unchecked so the list doesn't show on the stage. The game is about remembering the order of sounds in the list, so it's important that the player doesn't see the contents of the list.

3.

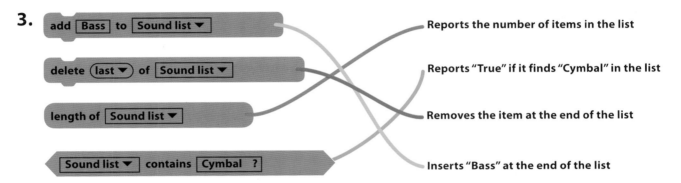

4. In the **delete** block, "**last**" should be "**all**," the **broadcast** message should be "**Add sound**," and the orange block should say "**set Level**."

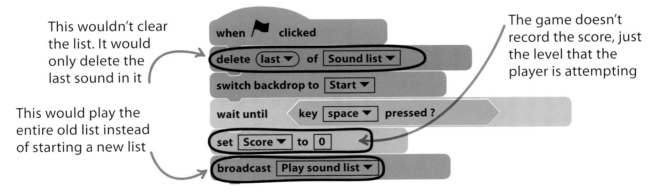

This wouldn't clear the list. It would only delete the last sound in it

This would play the entire old list instead of starting a new list

The game doesn't record the score, just the level that the player is attempting

5. Challenge! Copy the Drum-Bass sprite's scripts to the Drum-Tabla. Change the words and messages in the windows to match the new instrument, and choose which of its four sounds you prefer. Add an extra **if-then** block for the Drum-Tabla to each of the stage's two big scripts. Make sure you remember to change the **pick random** block so that its range is now **1 to 5**.

Getting Scratch

You can code online at the Scratch website, but if you aren't always connected to the Internet you can install Scratch on your computer.

I always use a mouse!

Scratch is easier to use with a mouse than a touchpad

Online Scratch

If you sign up for an account on the Scratch website, you'll be able to save your projects online and share them with friends.

1 Before you sign up to Scratch, get permission from a parent with an email address. Go to **scratch.mit.edu** and select **Join Scratch**. You'll need to set up a username and password. Don't use your real name as your username.

2 Once you've joined the Scratch website, click **Sign in** and then enter your username and password. Click **Create** at the top of the screen to start a new project. Happy coding!

Scratch 2

Offline Scratch

If you aren't always able to get online or you want to code offline, you'll need to download **Scratch 2.0** to your computer.

1 For the offline version of Scratch, go to **scratch.mit.edu/ scratch2download** and follow the installation instructions. The Scratch symbol will appear on your desktop.

2 To start Scratch, double-click on the **Scratch 2.0** symbol. When using Scratch offline, always save your work from time to time. (The online version saves automatically.)

Note for Parents

The Scratch website is run by Massachusetts Institute of Technology (MIT). It is intended to be safe for children to use. The instructions in this book are for Scratch 2.0, not the older Scratch 1.4. The online version of Scratch works well on Windows, Mac, and Ubuntu computers; the offline version isn't compatible with all Ubuntu versions. At the time of writing, the Raspberry Pi can't run Scratch 2.0. Help your child work logically through any coding difficulties. Check for obvious errors, such as mistaking similar-looking blocks for each other, and that scripts control the correct sprites. Remember: coding should be fun!